MONSTERS
UNDER
YOUR
HEAD

Written by Chad Sugg

MONSTERS UNDER YOUR HEAD
Copyright © 2008 by Chad Sugg

Cover design and layout by Chad Sugg
Photography by Jenna Winstead

Printed in the U.S.A.

ISBN: 978-1-312-08589-3

For you

When I mention to someone, whether it be a friend, stranger, family member, whomever, that I've written a book they always say the same thing, "Really? What's it about?"

My response is simply, "It's a poetry book... about everything."

And when I say that, I'm always a bit embarrassed, if only for the fact that the word *poetry* seems to be one people see as something 'only stuck-up, artsy folk write' or something 'only sad introverts write to avoid real life'. Up to this point in my life I'm quite sure I don't quite fit into either of those suits.

The following pages are nothing more than words I've put beside each other in an attempt to describe my ambitions, losses, hopes, faults, lies, loves, adventures and shortcomings, good days and bad, old friends, new fears, past, present, and what's to come.

I can assure you, I don't have the answers to anything in life... I only have my ideas. I can also assure you that answers aren't all there is to life. Too many people spend their life looking for them, when instead of asking themselves questions they should be asking their friends to come over.

The poems in this book are all as I originally wrote or typed them. The only revisions made were for spelling errors. I wanted this to be completely untouched by the hands and eyes of others to make sure it was in its original form. I didn't write these poems to be critiqued or judged on English, I wrote them to be read. I wrote them to be enjoyed and discussed with friends. I wrote them for my own enjoyment and release. I wrote them to give hope to that skinny kid from the shitty little town in that one state where no one visits. I wrote them to give a voice to the things people think but are too afraid to write.

I wrote these poems in the span of the last few years. Some are from scribbles in my notebooks, some from late nights in California when I missed the view of stars amongst streetlights in the Tennessee twilight, some from days in states I never thought I would see, some from drunken stupors on the keys of my computer, and some from times when I wished I had never learned the word 'why'.

When I started writing this Foreword I wanted it to have an insightful ending that brought the whole idea of this book together in nothing more than a paragraph. I wanted it to give the person reading it the same feeling I got when I walked out of the theater with a sudden burst of energy for life after seeing *The Pursuit Of Happyness*. I wanted it to give them the feeling of hope I got when I would sing Jimmy Eat World's "The Middle" in my head walking the hallways freshman year of high school when I was too depressed to admit I was actually depressed. But this is my first attempt at writing a poetry book and I can only hope that my attempt to evoke emotions with words on a page will work. So to wrap up the Foreword this is what I came up with:

For some reason people are very open to asking me very personal and deep questions. I'm always second-guessing myself when I reply, and can only hope that my response will be what they're looking for. When they ask for relationship advice I try my best to give good suggestions. When they ask for writing advice I give it to the best of my ability. And when people ask me what life is about, I simply reply...
"It's a poetry book... about everything."

Table Of Contents

- Poem titles with a * beside them are actually songs from my endeavors in the art of music as an artist known as Backseat Goodbye. Feel free to find the songs, wrap your heart around them, and never let go.

Monsters Under Your Head

A Colorful Bloom of Temporary Lights in the Sky

Every day I wake up and wonder how long it will take the
world to forget me.
My face.
My name.
The scent of my skin.
Every sentence I wrote on the back of a page
in the middle of ghost towns.

I don't want to stay.
This drink is my friend.
And no I do not want to die right now.

Every person, place and thing
pretty much lives and pretty much stays
the same.

It's not like I'm making you listen,
but if you do
you're can sure as hell bet I'm going to do my best to
make you think about how
you
don't
think
enough.

Life is short and so is the word 'now'.
So the next time you're in the arms of a daydream
with a pop song about the future stuck in your head,
remember this...
you cannot kiss a song lyric.
No matter how many times you write it on a page
it will never kiss back.

I encourage you to love lyrics with all of your heart,
but don't fall in love with them.

Instead, you should sing them out loud to a person you
wouldn't mind waking up beside for the next 60 years.

If you don't agree, that's fine.
But like a colorful bloom of temporary lights in the sky,
we will all eventually fade.
Our rights and wrongs will become dirt and the ground will
be our new home.

I'll still think about you there, as well.

And please don't take any of this the wrong way.
I mean well, but sometimes it's necessary to have your eyes
opened when you're least expecting it.
Many of my favorite things came from the spontaneous
combustion of a half assed question.

In bedrooms and balconies
of the kings and queens
of castles in the sea
where the parking lot is filled with headlights
and a kid from Duluth,
I've found hope from kind gestures in a kingdom of losers.

So the next time you're in a car on your way back home
turn down a new road and enjoy the thrill of being lost in a
town you claim to know.
You'll find your way back, I'm sure of it.

And like a colorful bloom of temporary lights in the sky,

you will shine.

The Golden Age of Heroes and Dreams

The golden age of heroes and dreams
has turned to robbers and TVs.
Ghosts are shopping for birthday gifts
while the muse of better days is getting drunk off boxed wine.

Grocery stores are selling water by the gallon now.
If you ask me, that shit should be free.
It amazes me how someone can be robbed at gunpoint
200 feet from my bed and the only reason I even know it
happened
is because of the news.

Oh well,
at least the birds haven't got too tired
of us polluting their air
to stop singing to me in the mornings.

my body is a universe

A commercial just told me,
"Your body is a universe."
So, if my body is a universe,
does that make my mind a television,
or a carpet?
Because I've been walked on before
and sometimes all I want to do is turn my thoughts off.

Honestly though
my body's not what I would consider a universe.
It's more like a small car
that runs on blood and caffeine
and I'm a self-made, sarcastic, procrastination machine.
I can dress myself,
and undress another in under thirty seconds flat.
Imperfections are my forte'
but I won't bother you with that.

Me,
I'm a cardboard cutout of a light bulb in a daydream.
You can turn me off or on with one slide of your hand.
I'm an introverted
Saturday loving
5 year old
trapped in the body of a 20 something.
How's that for a hypothesis of a life you can buy with half a
soul and a pack of cigarettes?

Don't tell me I 'cannot' do something.
When I turned 21
I erased that word from the dictionary
made mistakes and learned the real right and wrong.

Just because it's the unknown
doesn't mean that it's scary.
When my friends followed in the single file line
to a life they'd forget
I decided to make my own line with no regret,
instead.

Michael Jordan & The Candy Necklaces

I love your outlook on life,
but as far as I'm concerned
Michael Jordan is still the best basketball player
ever.

You can change your mind all you want,
paint your walls a different color every year,
wear as many candy necklaces as your heart desires
but I'm going to keep my walls this color
until they fade

Hold on
I just got a call from a friend
and forgot what I was writing about

Now all I can think about is how much I don't like wine.
As much as I wish I did
I just don't see the up side to drinking something that doesn't
taste good.
People say it's an acquired taste.
I say it's a nice way to waste money on bitter fruit punch.

But like I was saying
(back on track now)
Stop re-painting your walls
they're pretty just the way they are

The Truth About Last Year's List

Believable like 'if only'
You sat there with a blank look on your face
Six hours worth of 'what ifs'
Summed up in a word we all call 'gone'
Rain fell soft like concrete
So we covered our heads and hope for the best
Crossed fingers and bare-blocked crosswords
Met the summer with a handshake and a grin
Covered in children's clothing
You killed off all the bad dreams
It was easier than you thought
Now you breathe because you can
The doctors claimed a miracle
You quickly shuffled backward
Said, "Sorry, but no God held my hand.
If anything, thank the sunlight
and all the songs sung in my head.
I may be young,
but I've still got lungs
and a few good friends."

The flowers we got you had all wilted
by the time you got back home,
but you still put 'em on a shelf
and called them beautiful.

Trashcans Can't Fly

I'd like to thank you for your roofs
And all the adolescent words
That you handcrafted out of magic
Just to throw away in holes made of plastic

I'd like to wish you the best
On all the things you'll never guess
And the people that you meet
Are just the more you'll forget

I'd like to throw you a party
On an apartment balcony
So you can look down at the ground
And realize what it does for you

I'd like to spend all my money
On cookbooks, life books, and how to not worry
But first I'll have to learn how to read again
I'll forget how when age takes my eyes

I'd like to thank you for your blankets
And your excuses for the crash
Just because you love something
Doesn't mean it will last

But really,
Why make something last when the last thing you want is to
live in the past?

Raindrops (Clouds On A Couch)

love, like a inexcusable daydream
left on the corner for everyone to see
alive still though, alive and well
calm, every night and for the time being
interrupted so politely on a saturday, it seems
like raindrops, we fall
like raindrops, we fall

hold hands instead of hearts
like children's laughs on rooftops
we are vibrant and mistakably understood
with no use for words
no use for time and everything between

shout, fears you hide under walk-in closets
flashlights shine
you thought you had lost it
but there stands the past
to the right, toward the back

go ahead and cry
if we weren't meant to,
we wouldn't be able to...
right?
right.

right the wrongs and sing along
to the storybook ending of the movie script song
to the sound of the cars and the treetops' handclaps
to the drive in movie and the ground that collapsed
there's only so long something can be walked over
so step lightly, footsteps can be oh so deadly

close books and eyes
doors and lies
there's a reason for reasons
for you and i
to make like stars, and fall
like raindrops, we fall
like raindrops, we fall
but somehow,
somehow we make our way
back up to the clouds, somehow
somehow

The Green Winter

Did you ever stop
to think
That one day
you won't be alive
And the grass is only green
'til winter fills its lungs
Then it
dies

It's a sad
sentimental cycle
Of love, lies,
and light
That's swallowed
by the black hole
In the
sky

I keep telling you
to thank the night
For its warm subtle welcome
and goodbye

You never notice anything
'til it's gone

I Love The Future

If the wind wasn't blowing
you'd think the clouds were running.
I wonder if they're late for something?

If the sky was falling
you'd think the world was ending.
Maybe it would just want someone to catch it.
Falling is easier when you're not alone.

If the night was fading
you'd think the stars were hating
themselves for not being brighter than the sun.
They don't know the sun sometimes hates itself, too.

If the future was singing
you'd think today was leaving,
but it's not, because
tomorrow's just a new version of today.

Old Clothes Atlantic

you're standing in the doorway
i'm shivering cold, worried about the car ride over
your sister brought your old clothes
i'm sure the Atlantic can't wait to have you
don't forget to set your clocks back
and please call me when you get there
i'll leave the light on every night
just in case if you get scared
the look in your eyes was timeless
when i said those words
"i won't say goodbye,
but please know i love you"
winter had left the windows frostbit
so i drew some dreams i had on the ones facing the parking
lot
the sunrise reminded me of your smile
and how the photos could never make up for it
you say it's just miles and a few months
"i'll be back before you know it"
well i'll be waiting here on purpose
so don't you leave me guessing too long
darling, don't you go
the months have faded slowly but surely
the moonlit balcony hasn't been the same
i've left the doors unlocked just hoping
that maybe you might get back early
i haven't slept a wink for eight weeks
the voices outside calm me down
i've done my best to miss the sunsets
because i miss you, my morning sunshine from the west
please come home soon

Dream Of Waking Up

Real dreaming doesn't happen while you sleep.
No, no. My friends,
it's while you are awake.

Real dreamers can't sleep.
They lie awake at night.
Their minds racing, not only with the former day
but with the days and years to come.

One reason I know I'm truly in love with my own dreams
is because the reason I even try to sleep
is so I can wake up again.
To fight for them.
To keep them alive.
To keep myself alive.

Without my dreams I would be nothing
and a person without dreams
is nothing I'd want to be.

if you're a good kid
you'll study and believe in god
you best look both ways,
oh I almost forgot
if you do it all wrong, son.
you'll burn in hell.
these are the words I grew up with
in my town it was religion
or you were the devil
and it still is,
and I still wonder when they're going to realize
that god isn't some man in the sky
it's the people you love,
it's your lovers soft eyes
just after you made the best of your day
by sleeping in and leaving the tv off, for once.
don't tremble because they hate you
thrive because they just don't understand it.
you've got everything and everyone you could ever need
wrapped in that sweater that keeps your arms warm
memories will keep you warm, too
be sure to hold on to those as long as your mind will let you.
and when you get too old to even remember your first kiss
burn all the photographs and make new ones
it's all right in front of us,
has been since the stars exploded
and even the blind could see if they'd just try hard enough
we don't need fairytales or worry
when we've got love and second chances.
so let's close our eyes
so we can open our ears.
the wind will answer all of your questions if you ask it

because see,
there are no answers
there are just more words made from letters
and the thought that we're right.
so just live, kid.
forget about forever
and the true love you want to find.
just remember to forget
and it will all find you.

A House Built Out Of Stars

There's a house built out of stars just up the road from my
apartment.
The people that live there never turn the lights on.
I guess they're too busy being someone they're not.
Or maybe they're just too bored to even care what reality is.

Their yard's made of clouds and they don't have a sidewalk.
No windows are needed if you live outside.
There's no need to run if you don't need to hide.
And no need to worry if at least you're alive.

There's a store made out of night up the road from my place.
When you walk in you're actually walking outside, if that
makes sense.
They don't sell anything but they do give away love.
It's beautiful if you need it and reassuring if you don't.

Its parking lot is painted the color of the sky, a brilliant blue.
No maybe is needed if it already happened.
There's no need to wait if you're already late.
And no need to hurry if you believe in fate.

you took your hand from the sky
said you were tired of doing someone else's job
then the moon fell and shattered on the ground
i said "i'm sorry for the last six months, it's not your fault
you're stronger than the sky"
the nights were darker 'til they put it back together
the days were brighter though
i thought so at least

i climbed the clouds with you
when it was time to take it back
it looked awfully heavy, but you just said
"relax, i'm just pretending to play God... it's a one time thing,
i promise.
besides, i can quit when i want."

and then the rain fell
onto our eyelashes
we closed our eyes on that Tuesday night
and held our hands together
but nothing ever happened and never will

you're as human as me
i'm as flawless as you
perfect is a word made up by a fool
you can't count on page to erase all your doubt
a few dollars won't make that broken heart any better
a flower can't heal time
but the truth can take lies from their pedestal and push them
to the floor
you can't prove you'll miss me if you don't stay
a picture's worth a thousand words

but your love is much more

we can say "one day" all we want
but i'd much rather it be "today"
you're on tip toes waiting for the sunlight
and i can't wait for this rain to go away

Campus Crossing

The parking lot's empty by noon.
Balconies are left to clean themselves
As proof of yesterday's existence is swept from
their floors by the unknowing gusts of wind.
The flowers can't see the sun for the half empty beer bottles
and the chairs are hoping an afternoon rain shower
will rinse the spilled whisky from their armrests.
Half smoked cigarettes dance on the sidewalk
as if they survived the Holocaust.
All the while,
the college kids pass by on their way to the resident pool
where they won't actually swim,
but sit around the pool, instead.
The girls with fake tans will confuse the shirtless boys'
cockiness for being cool.
And I'm just wondering how these 'men' manage to get so
much gel in their hair,
when they should more so be worried about how much
they're going to hate themselves
when they're 30 and realize how shitty their skull tattoos
actually are.

She Rides Whales In Her Spare Time

I know you can't stand that your last name rhymes with your
first, but could you please tell me you still like my smile.
I begged the skyscrapers for shade,
but it's Monday, so they couldn't hear me very well for the
scrape of the pedestrians shoes on the concrete.
They must have thought I was begging for rain,
because it started to around noon,
but stopped when the flowerbeds began to complain.
I never knew roses were so rude.

I saw the weatherman from Channel 5 through a window
and I could swear he was holding strings that were attached
to the clouds,
which were attached to the sky, which was blue for the first
time (in minutes).
I asked him what he was doing and all he said was "Lying."
I misunderstood him and thought he said 'flying'.

About 5 minutes later I ran into you and you didn't even
notice me, so I said your name until you turned around.
When you did I heard a man behind me gasp.
Before I could push you out of the way the car was on top of
us. All I could see was your face and the dented underside of
an axle.

There were people screaming but it sounded like singing.
And for some reason you wouldn't stop smiling.
You told me you loved me and talked about how much you
liked orca whales until both our eyes closed
and the singing stopped.

Curtain Call

god came down in the middle of the day
a kid with a camera caught it all on tape
everyone was clapping, singing songs of glory and praise
they didn't seem to notice wires hanging from the clouds
the lights were too bright but they made it worth while
'cause it was kinda like a movie where the curtain call raises
the crowd
lightning bolts fell like rain from above
but they were just effects so no one got hurt
it's funny just to think that maybe, just maybe we're all
wrong
so you can read your books and i'll question all the words
i'm not saying you're a liar but the proof is no good
for me, maybe i'm just too naive.
but at least i'll admit i'm flawed
yeah i've a pointed a finger or pushed off the blame
but the reasons that you're breathing they just ain't the same
as you say
you can't pray for truth with those lies in your hands
i love you
but you're afraid of saying that back
just because i don't believe in all the same fairytales as you
doesn't mean i'm so bad
the future's all you have if you forget the past
so why not forgive and make the memories last
it's not up to me or a bible tale
you're the one that moves your feet
so you can follow any path, road sign or white lie
stumble forward, fall in love, chase the clouds, close your eyes
anything anyway you want, just don't let me or a book
someone else wrote make up your mind
you can't pray for truth with a lie in your hand

you don't need a miracle to save a life
you'll never be able to relive yesterday
so go ahead and enjoy today while you can

But You've Still Got The Ground

big trees and little kids
sunsets and katydids
love in the curve of your arms
silhouettes and somewhere else
sewn up in a memory
vibrant like a paint by number set

two plus two
and four by fours
stacked up like it's the end of the world
they say they're coming to take your name
but you're stubborn like a summer storm
and you don't really like the sound of change

especially when nobody knows who to blame
or what time the end even starts
so we'll stand like statues in the middle of a park
with a smile
and our hands on our hearts
failure on posters in the shadow of a man
copy cats in tattered hats
holding out their hands
waiting for a thanking from the people passer-bys
singing songs about dying
but the only words used are 'why'
paper hearts and homemade scarves
sitting on a shelf
watching through the window
but they could use some help
so won't you dust off those insecurities
and give them some air
today's just another

and childhood was nice
but now you're stuck in a face
that you forgot
when really's not nearly as bad as it seems
especially when nobody knows why they came
or what time the beginning began
so won't you sit up it's time to go
but don't you give up
because for all you know
tomorrow you could die
or peace could be found
your love made be lost
but you've still got the ground
so just push your feet
and go find someone else
'cause there's only one way
to say I love you
but there's so many people
you could say it to

Ballroom Dancing and the Past

I don't know about you
but I've got plans and dreams too
You can find me in my room
any night of the week

I've got high hopes
and a bottle of something
If all else fails
I'll drink this night away

If you're ever in the street
just think about life
And all that comes up
is the question "Why?"
Just know there's a difference between
funny and impossible

Improbabilities, foreign cities,
late night movie rental stores
Girls kiss the out of town boys,
boys kiss all the out of town girls
When it's late and they know
they should really be getting home,
but it's not like it's the end of the world
if they don't

We're gonna be alright
Here's to another Wednesday night
that we probably won't remember
twenty years from now

If you're ever in the grass

just thinking about life
And all that comes up
is the question "Where?"
Just know there's a difference between
distance and simplicity

Consequences, passing glances,
ballroom dancing and the past
It's easy to make a memory,
it's a little harder to take them back.

Why Wyoming?

It's a minute past yesterday
I'm lying under store bought sheets
There are people on my tv screen
Living lives made of lies

Is my ceiling fan happy?
Since it's still, I can't quite tell
My hair's so damn annoying
I'm thinking of cutting it again

It's funny how this full size bed
Can leave me so empty
But I am still breathing
Some consider that lucky

My walls look awfully lonely
Pasty white and rough like Wyoming
Starlit skies hide behind the clouds
Outside my window, beneath my blinds..
where the college kids laugh too damn loud

I was cold 10 minutes ago
Now I'm warm and a little bored
I think my bookshelf's smiling at me
My lamp's too dim so I'm not too sure
Maybe today the sun will shine
And I just might call up my Dad for once
I've some books under my bed
But they don't do me too much good there

Swallow The Sun

It's February and I just want April
To take my hand and pick me up again
Yeah I'm numb, but it's really not that bad

Love life 'til you get it wrong
Take a breath and turn your head
Oh my god I've gotta get out of this trend

It's 8:00 in the middle of a last chance
Can't we just pretend we don't know
Anything or anyone or anywhere anyway
It's kinda scary in the dark in the dim light
Can't I just pretend I don't mind
Everything or everyone or everywhere anyway

I've got a lot of life and you've got nothing
Don't swallow the sun
The moon isn't bright enough
We're all like flashlights
Useless 'til you turn us on
Sex and cigarettes are real
the apocalypse is Fate
replace the "t" with a "k"
Religion's a reminder
that our past is filled with liars

I spell my name with capital letters
But I don't talk much 'cause I'm a beginner at this life thing
Yeah I'm young, but that don't mean much here
If everyone knows that they're gonna grow old
Then why do we act like why we don't like the past?
If we had the chance we'd do it all over again

I've spent 21 years
Replacing my old fears for new ones
I've asked why, how, and where?
More times than I care to remember
I've got 7 days 'til a new week comes
And 24 hours to convince myself I'm real
'Cause today I'm not so sure I even exist

Sitting by the sinners on a bad day
Everybody's kiss is contagious
I'm tired of watching wars on my TV screen
There's not an easy way to say this
Nobody likes a winter
Sitting on the wind while the trees get thinner
Can't you just pretend you're a good kid?
Can't I just pretend I really give a shit
Even though I don't really know how I want to live?

I promise I'll be a better person this time next year.

if you're reading this...
congratulations, you're alive.
if that's not something to smile about,
then I don't know what is.

Lost In Love

you've got two left feet
and a way with words
you're in love with the "spottless mind"
but the ending's no good
you've got an eye for luck
along with black and white photographs
not too fond of windy nights
but you could spend all day laying in the grass
staring up toward the sky
hoping to skip with the sunset

you're such a sucker for a sad song
"summers always too long"
sitting in a swingset
trying just to sing along
with the song you've had stuck in your head since this
morning

here's to 3,2,1s and plastic guns
living in this city just ain't no fun, without you
and your lack of consequence
so wrap me up in your sympathetic sighs
saturday mornings and sweet white lies
i'm gonna pass out in the passenger seat
talk to keep you awake, 'til i fall asleep
and you'll laugh out loud at the irony of light
and the lack there of when you close your eyes
close them tight

lost in love
but it's better than none
i'm looking to fall asleep in your arms

here's a kiss on the cheek to you, from me
and one on your hand, so you can dream
and two on your sides, so you won't cry
and so you know, when you wake up
it's all gonna be alright.

Trees Have A Weird Sense Of Humor

This tree keeps waving at me like it knows me,
but I'm pretty sure we've never met.
I walked up and asked its name,
it just stood there like a lawn chair on its side in an un-
mowed front lawn.
I pulled a leaf from it,
and it asked why the hell I would do such a thing.
When I offered to tape it back on
                    it laughed and said it was kidding.

Virginia

well virginia came down the stairs
said "i have something to say, i love you anyway"
i opened my eyes and blew a kiss from the old couch
we found on the side of the road
this apartment has dirty steps
and a few broken windows
but it's the only place i could ever call home
i used to know your first name
but forgot it twice on purpose
when you said you had to go
it's not like the summer lasts all year
july left me here without you
the sun is gone, the stars all fell
i can't get to sleep tonight
and if you were here
it would all be alright
i told you not to laugh
when i said you looked beautiful
but you did it anyway
our old friends all left this town
but we liked the sound of it
so we just stayed
let's dance let's dance around the yard
clap our hands until we are gone

The Buildings Wept, I Walked

good morning kid
it's time for the world to end
grab your shoes
and don't worry about being late
halleluiah, we're still young
how are you now that you know the truth?
call it as it is
blame it on coincidence
pour your cup
one sugar or two
the sky's full of clouds
you're a glass half empty kind of kid
tomorrow's just a bother
today's always so nonchalant
you always wonder
why it has to rain when you dress up
figuratively speaking
you should have spoken up sooner
the bad guys won,
the buildings wept as you walked away
sidewalks shouldn't have this much influence
on where I've been or where I want to go
I can't remember your name
but could you kiss me
so I know I'm alive
you can even walk me home
so I'll forget what got me here
in the first place

calm down.
love me for all that I am and never will be.
call me out on those short comings.

kiss my laughs when I'm not looking.
draw sunsets over rainclouds and make them all fall down.
it's not today you wanted if yesterday is where you woke up.
I stopped running and started asking.
When is 'why' going to leave the sky?
and tell me you won't.
and tell me "I never."
breathe again!
oh my god!
the sky isn't dead
and I'm still alive!
if it's tonight I'm looking forward to
then why do I close my eyes?
draw sunsets under upsets
and give the light to the rest.
cough up the forgiveness and leave out the 'no I didn'ts'
this is another February and I'm another liar.
I don't have brothers, but do love my sister.
tell them I'll miss them when I can't call as often.
goodbye.
if I.
don't wait.
don't for a second forget the seconds.
it's time we're chasing.
so be it that I can't keep up.
it's too damn fast and there was never enough.
T for tomorrow.
I for isn't.
it just isn't for ME.
the sunlight.
it's finally,
oh my fucking god,
it's finally back in my arms.
summer, i've missed you.

you won't have to wait for me to ever kiss you again.
let's dance this dance,
who cares when it ends.
who cares when it ends.
who cares when it.....

Where is the wall that has love on it?

Excuse me,
but where is the wall that has love on it?
I've been looking for days and can't see a thing.
I can't find it tomorrow, if I give up today.

These maps are all wrong and simply confuse me.
Everyone else seems to know what they're doing.

So why me?
Why now?
Why this year, again?
If you studied my past you could call it a trend.
Of this one, that one, her, and her.
Why can't
I seem
To be
Me without you
In a world made of new.

New light, old lives,
Clean car windows
And parking lot wives.

I don't want everything.
Not by any means, at all.
I'm just tired, so tired,
Of sleeping alone.

Tiny Blue Shoes

The light lit up your face
You were 8 years old
Momma walked down the staircase
Daddy was cold
You pointed to the ceiling
Said, "We gotta fix it."
Then the clouds came through
Thank god the storms couldn't fit
You ran to the kitchen to find me
I had drawn you a picture of a flower or something
You grabbed a bag from a drawer
As tears from your eyes made their way to the floor
Your tiny blue shoes made marks on the linoleum
But you didn't mind, since true love's hard to find
You might as well use it

As you made your way to the living room, bag in hand
I said I was sorry, but don't worry
I know I forget sometimes
But I'll never...ever mean to hurt you again

The way you talked the clouds down was lovely
Then you shoved them in the bag and called them all ugly
Skipped through the room to the back door
Threw the ugly clouds out and said, "Please,
don't come back anymore."
You turned to us and said,
"Well tonight, we're gonna sleep,
we're gonna sleep all safe and sound."

You kicked your shoes off and kissed your own hand
I asked you why you were so brave

All you said is that you had never heard that word
but you were just tired of seeing all of us scared

Still Life

parted lips, two eyes too tight
remember all of the lines
it's so hard to keep a straight face
when i'm talking to myself
sunset in a solemn way
headlights on the overpass
if it gets worse you don't have to stay
any longer than you please
sit tight, don't make a move
you were always one to let it come to you
sometimes that doesn't work
sometimes you gotta stand up and shake that ass
false hopes in a well lit room
dead dreams on a photograph
i could let it get to me like it gets to you
but i think i'll leave it in the past
you can't blame me
for giving up so fast
new lies won't stop the crowd
it's just another thursday night
but i'm gonna grow out my hair
throw yesterday to the wind
i'm gonna move out west, leave this still life
new shoes on an old wood floor
you're counting on the next ten minutes
gonna stop time, gonna get the girl
but this isn't television, kid
brown eyes in a white walled room
colorblind with a thing for music
you say "love" is your favorite word
but you never find the time to use it
scraped knees in some new old jeans

you bought 'em at a store downtown
they don't make you any younger
but you like how they feel
on the skin that you hold so close
insecure, but you think no one knows
what it's like to want to live and die at the same time
you can't blame me
for giving up so fast
new lies won't stop the crowd
it's just another thursday night
but i'm gonna grow out my hair
throw yesterday to the wind
i'm gonna move out west, leave this still life
new words on a plain white page
old songs on the radio
found love on friday night
to think you didn't want to go
touched lips on another's skin
small words in a big blue sky
i hated life before i found that song
now everything's alright
you can't blame me
for giving up so fast
new lies won't stop the crowd
it's just another thursday night
but i'm gonna grow out my hair
throw yesterday to the wind
i'm gonna move out west, leave this still life

Remember When We Threw Fireworks At Mom And Chris?

I didn't know what I was going to do
I just knew there was no way in hell I was going to let you get
past me

The drive there was beautiful
I remember this because we said it so many times to each
other in the car.
We parked and I took a photo of a frowning tree
with my new old Polaroid I bought at Goodwill the week
before

All of our feet were slipping as we descended the hill
but the cave got closer with each step.
so we kept going

We were almost there when you both fell
I didn't know what I was going to do
I just knew there was no way in hell
I was going to let you fall past me

I used all of the strength in my body.
I slammed my foot into the ground so hard to stop us from
sliding farther
that I broke one of my toes.

After I stopped you
I noticed I still had my arms sprawled out
just in case.

As we climbed the hill back to the car
The pain set into my foot and ran up my leg

It felt like the rocks and roots had turned into glass
And with each step I took I tried harder and harder to keep
from showing
that by saying I was alright, I actually wasn't.

You kept saying you were sorry to the both of us
And we repeated that it was alright
When we made it to the top of the hill
I could see what was left of the daylight

I thought you were getting in the back of the car
but it was then when I realized you were just getting the door
for me.
People never get the door for me.
It was nice.

On the way back to our apartment
I replayed what had happened over and over again in my
head.
The only time I stopped was to tell your mom "you're
welcome."

You told him and me you were glad you were with us
And it was then when I realized after we had all lived together
for almost three years
that in a month you two would be riding in that car without
me in the back seat.
To a town three hours away
where I won't be able to have your cigarette smoke follow me
even when the wind is blowing in a different direction.
I never thought I'd miss my clothes smelling like cigarettes I
hadn't smoked.

I thought wrong.

Denying Death On A Hotel Bed

I guess my eyes are going out
'cause I can't seem to see you anymore

Sure they told me you died
but I don't have to believe if I don't want to

Swingset Song

two kids are on a swingset
outside by me and you
and i can't quite place where i placed my keys
the sun is setting the moon is bright tonight
and i love the shadow our hands cast by the trees
the leaves don't fall anymore 'cause it's summer thank god for
that
and i could run away, i've got legs for that
but i've got a home now and i like it here
the birds outside my door
sing me to sleep i'm sure
to thank them every night and keep in touch
with the friends i thought i'd lost somehow i always find them
where i left them
i'm beginning to think my parents were right all along
i used to be scared of love
but now i keep it close, without it we would all forget to
breathe
fairly soon i want to move to a small house on the coast
just because the ocean's so damn pretty
like a flower pedal lost in the wind's relentless gust
i've forgotten where i'm from but still have hope
that i'll find myself a new life not too different from the old
where i'll laugh and get lost some more
and we'll still have inside jokes
and i'll still be so forgetful
and we'll trade in all our money for the simple things
they say dreams are uncertain
i say lies are overrated we should bury them and smile a little
more
'cause if there's one thing i've learned
from being young and insecure

it's you don't need no money to live and be happy
just find some friends and forget all the worst

2:16 am

I just heard the movement
of my own feet
as they brushed across the carpet

I don't know why
but the fact
that I could hear
and feel
this action
amazed me
and made me
glad to be alive.

Don't Judge A Werewolf By Its Cover

Judging from the sounds outside my window right now,
you'd think there was a werewolf
playing basketball in the parking lot.
But if you look out my blinds,
you'll just see my old crazy neighbor howling,
and a drunk kid dribbling a volleyball.

My Favorite Color

i collect sunsets in the palm of my hand
you stomp out the moonlight every chance you get
one day you're gonna want them back
when you do i'll turn my head

you're the good luck for my bad ideas
i'm the covers on your bed
you're my dreams when i can't sleep
and i thank you for that
i'm you're wednesday evening's afternoon
you're a store sign blinking on and off
you say time it's just a waste of light
"i give you love, 'cause you're all i've got"

it's a common misconception
to wanna get the best of a worse situation
falling back on unpredictable scenarios
will get you nowhere so turn up your stereo
well you've gotta get out soon
and no no
you won't know where to
but you're sure as hell gonna get out of this town
put that pedal to the floor
clap those hands to the beat.
don't know where i'm headed
but i'm getting out of Tennessee

you're a candle in the coldest room
i'm a children's storybook
you open me every chance you get
my cover is your favorite color and i love it how you look...
out the window and up the stairs

and talk to yourself when no one's there

love is such a simple word,
but i'm glad to be in it with you

and we can laugh all we want
i know it's your favorite
and i'll stare at you all i can,
'cause you...
you're my favorite

Drive Tomorrow Off A Cliff

drive tomorrow off a cliff
and if you start to feel sick
remember yesterday was just a day too
and today was what you made it
people die, people kiss
some kids love, other just miss
chances, hopes, dreams and night skies
moonlit walks only last 'til you...
why is it that i can scream it in my head
but stand mute with unmoved lips
when it comes to staring you in the eyes
ballroom talk can call it quits
it's Wednesday night and I'm alive
alive, or a liar?
composure comes first
leave last and think fast
first moves are the worst
if I'm not wondering if it's mutual
i'm busy counting clouds
or times I could've and would've
but didn't and should've
this is just a
i was just a
no, no, can't say that here
it's a nice day
and you're a nice kid
but hell, I'm too damn worried
about a consequence
so fuck it
tomorrow's Thursday
and I've seen so many
so why am I so surprised

to wake up with no beginning
people lie, people wish
some kids run, others just stand there
wondering if a moonlit walk
will ever even come their way

I was standing by a tree in Michigan, while the folk band played a slow song

Yesterday
a little girl
passing by
waved, smiled and said 'hi'
to me.

I smiled about it afterward
for at least 20 minutes,
and wondered at what age
that nice little girl will
stop
waving, smiling and saying hi
to unsuspecting people
that really need those simple gestures sometimes
just so they know the world isn't ending quite yet.

I hope it's no time soon

Encore! Encore!

epically forgotten
wearing next to nothing
the lights keep telling you otherwise
you made it this far
but beginnings don't tell the truth
your best friends are the worst liars
so i'll be waiting for the encore
give it your all, they're all watching now
collapsed, repeated, beat down, deceited
it's the middle of the night where are you?
i can't say i'm too surprised
if it's nevermore then go to hell
i'll see you when i get there, on the other side
of what was never meant to be
do his lips taste sweet like wine?
and does he kiss you in the middle of the night?
when your voice gone from all those shots
pretty's just a point in time
i hope the memory of the lies you keep
haunts you 'til you die
so i'll be waiting for your "i'm so
sorry this is not the way i meant to be,
it's just that sometimes it's hard for me to sleep or even tell if
i'm alive
well welcome to the real word
your television's nice but only tells you lies
yeah the grass is green but there is no other side
and you can count the days all you want
but they're never gonna add up
your life isn't a problem
you just don't know how to live it right

Teenage Mutant Ninja Puddles

I always want to run through puddles after it rains,
but I never want to get my clothes wet.
So, I don't.

I remember when I was younger
I used to think the Ninja Turtles lived in the sewers
under my town.
There was a sewer mantle on the crosswalk in front of the old
Wal-Mart and I'd always tell my mom,
'That's where the Turtles live!"
as we walked by it.
There was no question about it,
my imagination allowed me to know for a fact that the pizza
eating turtles lived underground in my town...
it was such an awesome thing.

I also remember when I was that age
if I saw a puddle I wanted to run and jump in,
I didn't think twice about getting my shoes and socks wet.
So, I did.

I wish I was still as brave as I was back then.

How Does A Lion Tamer Fall In Love?

I would have to say
piano is the prettiest instrument I've ever heard.
I would also have to say
piano is the foremost instrument on my list of instruments I
would least like to have dropped on my head.
I don't actually have a list like that,
but if I did, piano would definitely top it.

But back to the question,
how does a lion tamer fall in love?
I would imagine he falls in love just like fireflies do.
As well as trees, buildings, me and you.
But why does he want to tame the lion?
Shouldn't he just let the lion go back to its actual home.

I'm sure the lion loves the luxury of the finest food and the
flat screen television in his dressing room,
but I bet no coffee on earth could taste as good to him as the
fresh waters of a small pond in a small dot on a big map in
Africa.
He probably really misses his lion buddies back home,
but no one ever asked him if he wanted to travel the globe.
They just kind of tied him up in a box made of metal in the
back of a truck.
Now he's much older and the only trees he ever sees are made
of plastic with rubber leaves.

I Think I Might Change My Name To Tomorrow

Well how about that, it's a matter of fact
The life you got is all you'll get
You better do your best not to fuck it up too much
Yeah the thing about that is it's the truth you lack
And you can smoke until your lungs turn black
The Surgeon General couldn't really give a shit less

Seasons change and people stay the same
Each year the whores hike their skirts up a bit more
We're all just numbers on a cartoon calendar page
We listen to the music, but it's the lyrics that we all ignore

Well how about that, it's a matter of fact
You retraced the words that you never said
Now you're staring out at a useless blank canvas
Yeah the truth about that is you're the one who said
I'm gonna change myself, become a better person
"No, I swear, I really mean it this time."

Years they fade, my memory takes the blame
Each night the girls spread their legs just to make more
We're all just actors in an ad for the American Dream
We the people just want peace, but our countries just want
to make war

Everybody everywhere has thought the same things you have
So don't be afraid to fall in love with a stranger
Everyone on every street is free to use their body as they
please
So don't be afraid to take some chances once in a while

Here's the part where you start to think

That you don't believe in anything
Words are just words and you're just drunk
Here's the part where you start to act
Like you're better off without the things you have
Once they're gone you'll realize you fucked up again

Seasons change and people stay the same
Each year I find a new way to lie a bit more
We're all gone just as fast as we came
So I'm not counting on a new life,
No no no, Tomorrow here I come

Darling, you're lovely, but you're awfully naive
Did you think about when your future might leave ya?
You can't buy the sky, yesterday's not for rent right now,
Go find your own forever somewhere else
Next year's accepting applications
For one night stands and New Years Resolutions
But don't forget what you got right here
My smile's sometimes fake, but me, I'm real

Stop debating wars, politics and freedom
We're all human last time I checked
If you want to kill a man for the color of his skin
Then it's obvious to me that you're a goddamn idiot
We're all free to think the things we want
But you're too busy with your bullshit to hear us talk

So now here I stand, in the corner of my Past
and I don't want to go
'Cause it feels good to know what is and what was
And the Future's just a mirror that I lost for the fear of
Death and a life without Love
And just when I thought the world had ended

The Sun broke through the pitch black sky
In the most beautiful fucking glow I'd ever seen
The buildings started singing
and my fear finally left me
I shouted,
"Goddamn it feels good to be alive again!"

Cure The Silence

Light leaks through a lazy window seal
Eyes wake to a sky pouring rain
If love is love, and I'm alive
I guess I'll be okay
White walls wait for paint
Doors creak to cure the silence
Years passed lie in the grass
Of the fields I won't remember
And you, you're just waking up
Keep your head up kid
Don't look back, you say
There's only four more months 'til May
Then you can move out
And do as you please
I'm so sorry,
So sorry for saying sorry so much
And I beg of you
to please just keep in touch

Don't Read Books With Sunglasses On

Don't read books with sunglasses on.
Sure, it's fun at first,
but ultimately you'll just make yourself look like an ass.
And I can assure you that just because a pair of sunglasses
may make you LOOK cool,
that doesn't mean you ARE cool.

When I put on a pair of Ray Bans
the fact that I own three different versions
of each Star Wars movie
and sleep in Hanes boxers with patterns on them
doesn't vanish into thin air.

No, no...
even with my sunglasses on
I am the most un-cool person, ever.

The Ghosts Of My Own Are The Only I Know

I want to love you,
but it seems as if I'm the only ghost haunting this house right
now.

These walls are some of my best friends,
but when it's late and I'm like this they can say some pretty
harsh things.

We say times are hard,
when really we're just too dumb to notice change isn't a
name...
but more like a thing we're afraid to let stay.

I want to know you,
but it seems as if I'm the only person that drives these
interstates while every sane person in this town is asleep.

These roads all have names,
and I remember theirs, but they never seem to know mine.

We say life is hard,
when really it's easy, and we're just too numb to notice we've
only got one.

I want to love you,
but it seems as if I'm the only ghost haunting this house right
now.
I can open the doors on my own,
but who wants to go into a room where no one knows you?

Heaven, Hell And Tomorrow

they say that one day
the world's supposed to end
but i'm pretty sure it already did
i can see it in your eyes,
i can see it in the way you wave your hand
they say that one day
we will all see his face
but what about those of us who have all lost our faith
we traded in our bibles for the taste of sex and sweet of
untold sin
one day you learned how to spell heaven
the next you told me to go to hell
well it's the hypocrites that sink on ships
so i hope to see you smile when you go down
when you go down
oh no
oh oh no
look at that
all you have left is the past
one day you learned
how to spell forgotten
the next you left me with open hands
so i swore from that point on i'd always stand
alone like a boat or a well crafted star
in the middle of the ocean just as long as it's far
from your reach, you can't see
those words didn't mean...
a damn thing to you, but they meant the world to me
oh no
oh oh no
hand claps won't save you now
your love is just a lie

all you want is summer, but it's the middle of winter
and you hate the sound of "home"
they say that one day
we will all die alone
but what about those of us
who just refuse to go
we hate the thought of dying so we lie and say it won't come
they say that one day
peace will be present
but i don't see how
when we've got a liar for a president
the revolution's here,
we just have to stand
they say that one day
the world's supposed to end
but i'm pretty sure it already did
i can see it in your eyes,
i can see it in the way you wave your hand
oh no
oh oh no
hand claps won't save you now
your love is just a lie
all you want is summer, but it's the middle of winter
and you hate the sound of "home"
the night's too dark
the day's too light
either way you hate them both
it's not matter of getting out
it's the thought of nowhere to go
goddamn we did it again
we made though they said we wouldn't
goddamn we did it again
we made it though they left us for dead
i believe this calls for a celebration

so raise your glasses and calm your nerves
it's just a night like any other
but let's give them something to remember
i can't wait to wake up
to tomorrow
you wanted a miracle
well a goddamn miracle's what you're gonna get
well i'm gone for now
but not for good
yeah we're gone for now
but not for good
yeah it'll be a while
but you can bet i'll be back
just keep your eyes toward the sun
and this song in your head

keep your eyes toward the sun
and this song in your head

Today Was Today

Today is not my birthday.
Today I am not in love with a girl.
Today I didn't meet anyone new.
Today I overslept an hour or so.
Today I ate breakfast outside with the sun in my eyes.
Today not one person has knocked on my door.
Today I talked to myself and combed my hair.
Today I walked to the mailbox and nothing was there.
Today I am not the luckiest person I know.
Today I can't remember what time I woke up.
Today is not the best day of my life.
Today is not the worst day of my life.
Today is just a normal day, and I'm just fine with that.

Indifference in A-Flat Major

I played my piano for the first time in a while today.
I mean I REALLY played it.

There's nothing like the feeling of piano keys brushing against
your fingertips to make you forget you miss the old days.
The days when your bedroom walls were covered with
posters of the people you'd give anything to meet.

Oh if these walls could sing.
If these walls could sing they would sing a beautiful song.
It would ring throughout the parking lot.
And instead of the sound of cars and lights,
we would hear notes
and our own breath.

It would be beautiful.

Like the look on someone's face when they realize everything
is. going. to. be. alright.

Modern Love (Is Dead)

No. No. No!
No, it is not!
I refuse to believe it's not alive.
Hearts may not have eyes,
but they're sure not blind.

Give me every word you can
on how many times you've cursed your own name
for words you wanted to
but didn't ever say.

Subtract your own apathy.
We'll stack our hands like legos
and paint this whole town whatever color we want.
Something more pleasing to the eyes, though.
Because lately everyone here has been talking
about how Love is dead.
And I'm just not going to believe them anymore.

It's not like they ever believed it was alive in the first place.

Come Tomorrow

the kids are asleep
mom and dad are at the local bar
playing with each others hair
husband turns to wife, says
oh what a lovely evening we're having dear

then the ground fell beneath them
as the club poured to the floor
heaven help us we won't lie to ourselves or anyone anymore

i'm awake now
can you blame me for crying out loud?
you divorced when i was a baby
now i'm all grown up, look at me, i'm fine
all my life i was told maybe
maybe one day kid you'll grow up and be alright
well i never i never believed the words they'd leave on the
front steps
they seemed so bland and absent of sincerity

so one day i graduated
moved to a town two hours away
i figured maybe the kids would be different here
but it turns out their all the same
when will i ever get this right?
or will i ever get this right?

oh no i'm alone again
oh well that's the way it is
oh no i'm alone again
oh well guess that's just the way it is

come tomorrow
i'll wake up new
come tomorrow
i'll wake up new.

Monsters Are Afraid Of The Dark, Too

You can't have monsters under your bed
if your bed is a couch.
You can't have love
if you refuse to be loved.
You can't have a home
if you don't have a house.
You can't have peace
if you play with guns.

And actually,
You can have a home if you don't have a house.
Home can be anyone, anywhere, anything.
East, West, Tennessee, California.
I've found homes when I knew that I couldn't.

Because knowing you can or knowing you can't,
really just means you're right or a hypocrite.

You can't have too many friends.
You can't live too long.
You can't have too many favorite songs.
You can't ever love too much.

You can take things for granted though,
but don't
because even monsters need the simple things to breathe.

This Is What I Meant By Maybe

If we measure life
by how long it takes us
to get from point A to point B
We'll only end up at point C
Circle starts with the letter 'C'
and no one wants to go in circles
Unless, of course, you're in love
Then you could stand in one spot forever
Spinning in one constant motion
Wishing on nothing more than stars
And times like a minute after 11:10
A.M. or P.M., it doesn't matter which
Without love you look for both times
And sometimes even cheat and wish twice
If you catch it on two clocks
That are running a little late or early

If we measure life
by how many teaspoons it takes to get drunk
We'll end up breaking bottles in tube socks during winter
Making sense is something you don't care about
When you've lost the ability to forget
And as humans it's easier to just act like it never happened

BUT
It did happen
And our brains are like elephants and NEVER forget
Unless of course it was something insignificant
Though significance can only be told by how bad you want it
to happen again
And again and again,
Until you've forgot what it's like to remember high school

When you were to young to give two fucks about whether or not tomorrow was Tuesday or Wednesday

No matter how old I get
Weekends are something I'll always look forward to.

Calico Kitten

If my life had a soundtrack it would be acoustic
With songs about the way I laugh
at my ability to love things that I can't have

If my life were a movie
It would be black and white
with still-frames in color and hue
The credits would say a simple phrase, like
"You aren't what you say or what you do,
so don't worry so much,
just get on with a life that you love"

I had a good day
Since I didn't die or have to wait
In any really long lines at the store
Me, I like to make music
You just like to make war

There's a calico kitten prancing across a rooftop
Smiling at the grey withered sky
He's watching all the cars as they pass by
Their blinkers go click click click
This new height makes him homesick
He misses his mother the most
And his long days by the window
They're long long gone

If you're alright, then I'm alright
If you're alright, then I'm alright

It feels good to be alive again

So good to see the sky again

I Drew You A Picture Of A Plant So You Wouldn't Have To Water It

You're like a forgetful, accidental Hitler when it comes to
plants.
But I know you mean well.

You always forget to water them.
And you always feel bad when you find them all dead.
So, last night I didn't buy you a new one.
I drew you a picture of a plant instead.

It's pretty and green
with shiny crayon leaves.
You can name it and frame it,
whatever you please.

Burn it, love it,
throw it away.
Forget it, water it,
sit it in shade.

It's yours.
I made it.
Just for you.
A smile.
Or a laugh.
Is the least you could do.

Head In The Clouds

you said
"hey kid, there's nothing for you up in them clouds.
so why do stare and sing so loud?"

i don't know but one day that sky's gonna fall down,
and i'll be just fine.
i'll be singing at it's side.
and you can run all you want
you'll get nowhere fast
there's a reason for those lungs kid
once they're used up, you can't give 'em back
so don't look back, 'cause you'll regret
those rainy days you can't forget
that sunday morning's afternoon
the one you lost and the look they gave you
summers spent in southern towns
the matinee and your mother's gown
and how you used to have a reason
to wake up

and i can't say that i fully comprehend your reasons
for giving up
you can say whatever you please, but don't blame it on luck
this isn't high school kid, this is real life...
live it how you want to
but don't bother coming back to this town
every time you're lied to

living in the city just ain't so pretty at night
when you look up you can't see a god damn star in the sky
and it's not like you asked for this
but it's not like anyone cares

and i'll sing how i like
with my head in the sky
yeah i'll sing how i like
with my head in the sky

I'm Tired Of Today

I'm giving up on love.
My head's a ceiling and my heart's a rug.
The girls on that balcony don't even know my name
(And I'm sure they don't want to.)

I'm giving up on light.
Changing back to a skin that feels right.
I'm not me any more than I used to be.

I've stopped knocking on doors.
Sleep is all that makes sense anymore.
(And I'm pretty sure I still don't like to lie.)

I'm tired of today.
No matter how much I love it, or hate it.
It will still fade.

I kiss you in my mind sometimes.
That's as close as I'll ever get.

So this is me, moving on.
Onto a life where, if I have it, that's great.
And if I don't, that's just fine, too.

In The Pursuit Of Significance

Dearest Friend,
When the world ends, both of our ships will end up in the same sunken harbor. We will inevitably share the same fate, and no matter how great we become at living life we will forever remain as nothing more than just human. We were brought into this world unknowing of what we would find, where we would end up, or who we would become. You are as lost as me, and vice versa. As the winds of change blow in the new tomorrow I can only hope they'll allow us to catch up with it before it passes us by.

As humans, we posses certain abilities. The ability to love, to care, to hope, to dream, to cry, to beg, to die, to live, but most importantly, the ability to adapt. It's survival of the fittest in our world full of witches and cops, ATMs and parking lots, magazines and football games, sarcasm and taxes. Just when you think you're ahead you realize you're at the back of the line and you forgot your wallet at home. So I'll ask you now, though you may want to exercise your ability to become a shadow of your own thoughts, don't. Living isn't easy at times like this, but I can assure you that Father Time will soon guide you to clarity, and it's then when you'll remember how to smile.

Just because you can't see the horizon, doesn't mean it's not there. And when you do find it again, I'll be there waiting and we can set off on our ships made of insecurities, empty beer bottles, and duct-tape. Yeah, both our worlds will end eventually, but until then we can look at all the pretty lights, talk shit about the government, and get lost as much as we want. We might not ever amount to much in our own eyes, and I can bet we'll still be asking the same questions we do today twenty years from now. But at least when we're on our deathbeds years and years and years and years from now we can laugh about that time Garrett said "Storm's a broomin'..." and no matter whether it's eternal sleep, or Gods and Halos that wait for us after our stay here, at least we'll know we had a damn good time trying to figure it all out along the way.

Signed,
Chad Sugg

CHAD SUGG was born in Clarksville, Tennessee, and attended Middle Tennessee State University. He began writing at the age of 15 and self-released his first musical album under the name Backseat Goodbye in 2005. He began work on this book in early 2008.

Chad is currently 22 and resides in Murfreesboro, TN, where he continues to sing songs and scribble words on pages.

Monsters Under Your Head is his first published book of poetry.

CPSIA information can be obtained at www.ICGtesting.com
Printed in the USA
LVOW07s0248020215

425285LV00002B/119/P

9 781312 085893